Apr 2015

My Daily Diet: Dairy

On My Plate

Building a Healthy Diet with the 5 Food Groups

My Daily Diet: Dairy

My Daily Diet: Fruits

My Daily Diet: Grains

My Daily Diet: Proteins

My Daily Diet: Vegetables

On My Plate

My Daily Diet: Dairy

Rosa Waters

Mason Crest

Mason Crest
450 Parkway Drive, Suite D
Broomall, PA 19008
www.masoncrest.com

Printed and bound in the United States of America.

First printing
9 8 7 6 5 4 3 2 1

Series ISBN: 978-1-4222-3094-7
ISBN: 978-1-4222-3096-1
ebook ISBN: 978-1-4222-8787-3

Library of Congress Cataloging-in-Publication Data

Waters, Rosa, 1957- author.
  My daily diet : dairy / Rosa Waters.
      pages cm. — (On my plate)
  Audience: Age 9+
  Audience: Grade 4 to 6.
  Includes bibliographical references and index.
  ISBN 978-1-4222-3096-1 (hardback) — ISBN 978-1-4222-3094-7 (series) — ISBN 978-
1-4222-8787-3 (ebook) 1. Dairy products in human nutrition—Juvenile literature. 2. Dairy
products—Juvenile literature. I. Title.
  QP144.M54W38 2015
  613.2'6—dc23
                                           2014010564

Contents

KEY ICONS TO LOOK FOR:

Text-Dependent Questions: These questions send the reader back to the text for more careful attention to the evidence presented there.

Words to Understand: These words with their easy-to-understand definitions will increase the reader's understanding of the text, while building vocabulary skills.

Series Glossary of Key Terms: This back-of-the book glossary contains terminology used throughout this series. Words found here increase the reader's ability to read and comprehend higher-level books and articles in this field.

Research Projects: Readers are pointed toward areas of further inquiry connected to each chapter. Suggestions are provided for projects that encourage deeper research and analysis.

Sidebars: This boxed material within the main text allows readers to build knowledge, gain insights, explore possibilities, and broaden their perspectives by weaving together additional information to provide realistic and holistic perspectives.

Introduction

Most of us would agree that building healthy bodies and minds is a critical component of future success in school, work, and life. Providing our bodies with adequate and healthy nutrition in childhood sets the stage for both optimal learning and healthy habits in adulthood. Research suggests that the epidemic of overweight and obesity in young children leads to a large medical and financial burden, both for individuals and society. Children who are overweight and obese are more likely to become overweight or obese adults, and they are also at increased risk for a range of diseases.

Developing healthy eating and fitness habits in childhood is one of the most important gifts we can all provide to children in our homes and workplaces—but as any parent can attest, this is not always an easy task! Children are surrounded with both healthy and unhealthy eating options in their homes, schools, and in every restaurant or store they visit. Glossy marketing of food and meals is ubiquitous in media of all types, impacting both children's and adults' eating choices. As a result of the multiple influences on eating choices, from infancy through adulthood, we all benefit from additional support in making healthy choices.

Just as eating and fitness can become habits in adulthood, personal decision-making in childhood is critical to developing healthy habits. Providing healthy options and examples are a starting point, which can support children's healthy habits, but children also benefit from understanding the rationale for eating reasonable portions of healthy foods. Parents, teachers, and others often communicate messages through their words and actions—but books can provide more detailed information and pictures.

Building on this need for developing informed consumers, the ON MY PLATE series provides elementary school children with an informative yet fun introduction to their eating options. Beginning with an introduction to the five food groups, children can learn about what they ideally will have on their own plate and in their mouths. Tips are provided for choosing healthy snacks. And children will understand the importance of eating a range of foods. These books empower our children to make healthy decisions for themselves.

An additional benefit of this series may be the trickle-up effect for parents. Even if we all *know* the importance of making healthy choices for meals and snacks, there's nothing like a child *reminding us* why this is important. When our children start citing the long-term consequences of our dietary choices, we tend to listen!

Here's to developing healthy eating habits today!

Lisa Albers Prock, MD, MPH
Developmental Behavioral Pediatrician, Boston Children's Hospital
Assistant Professor, Harvard Medical School

WORDS TO UNDERSTAND

bacteria: Tiny life forms that are too small to see. Some bacteria make you sick, while others keep you healthy.

edible: Able to be eaten.

shelf lives: How long food stays good, without spoiling.

udders: The part of a cow that milk comes out of.

Chapter

1

Where Does Dairy Come From?

Milk, cheese, ice cream, and yogurt all have something in common—they're all dairy foods. And all dairy foods come from animal milk. Milk comes right from the animal. Cheese and other dairy foods are made by changing milk into another food.

Dairy foods also have something else in common. They all come from farms. Animals that produce milk live on farms, where they're milked. Without farms, we wouldn't have dairy foods—or many other foods for that matter.

THE ANIMALS

Most of the milk people drink comes from cows. Some people drink other animals' milk, though, like goat milk, camel milk, water buffalo milk, and sheep milk. A lot of the cheese and yogurt sold in grocery stores comes from sources other than cows. Feta cheese, for example, is usually made from sheep's or goat's milk.

MAKE CONNECTIONS

You may have heard of or even tried nondairy milk, like soymilk or coconut milk. Those foods are called milk because people tend to use them the same way. They add them to cereal, put them in coffee or tea, and use them to bake. They also look a lot like animal milk, but nondairy milk does not come from animals. Soymilk comes from soybeans, almond milk comes from almonds that are pressed so hard liquid comes out, and coconut milk comes from inside coconuts. Nondairy milk can be healthy and delicious, especially if you're someone who can't digest dairy milk.

Dairy is an important part of the American diet. Without it, we wouldn't have milk, butter, cheese, ice cream, and more—and it all starts with cows on a farm like this!

MAKE CONNECTIONS

You don't have to rely on factories to make all your dairy foods. One dairy food you can easily make at home is butter. First, buy some heavy cream. Pour the cream into a jar with a tight lid. Shake the jar for ten or more minutes. You have to be patient, and make sure you don't drop the jar! If you add a couple of clean marbles, the process will go a little more quickly. Or you can use a food processor or an electric mixer to beat the cream. Watch closely as you shake or mix. First, it will turn into whipped cream. As you keep shaking, it will suddenly separate into butter and a clear liquid called buttermilk. Once that happens, pour the contents of the jar over cheesecloth or a paper towel. Squeeze it until all the buttermilk drains out. Wash your butter with cold water, until the water runs clear. Then you're left with a solid mass of butter!

The cow milk we drink comes from farms. Many cows live together on one farm. Some dairy farms are small. One farmer has a few cows or a few dozen cows. They live on fields, where they eat grass. Farmers and farmworkers usually milk cows twice a day, once in the morning and once in the evening.

Other dairy farms are huge. They have tens of thousands of cows. On these farms, the cows usually live in barns rather than on fields. They are herded from their stalls to milking barns two or three times a day. They are mostly fed grains, like corn, rather than grass.

Today, most farmers don't milk cows by hand. Machines hooked to the cows' **udders** do the milking. Multiple machines can milk many cows at the same time. Machines allow farmers to have many more cows.

The milk from farms is collected into huge tanks. Trucks come every day to take milk from the tanks to the next steps.

PROCESSING

After the milk is collected, it has to be processed. That means farms and factories have to do things to the milk before it can be sold. Processing also means the ways in which milk is made into other dairy foods.

In most states, milk must be pasteurized before it makes its way to stores. Pasteurization is a method of heating milk to kill bacteria that might be growing in it and that could make people sick.

Some milk is used to make other dairy products like cheese or yogurt. It is taken to factories, where workers and machines make these foods.

To make cheese, for example, the milk is put into a vat and heated. In most cases, a culture (which is actually **edible bacteria**) is then added, and the milk is allowed to sit.

RESEARCH PROJECT

This chapter gives an overview of how cheese is made in a factory. Pick another dairy product—like yogurt, sour cream, or ice cream—and research how it is made. Write out a list of steps from the farm to the factory to you. Include transportation between each step, as well as the people who participate in each step.

The food that cows eat can have an effect on the flavor of their milk. Many people feel that milk from grass-fed cows is better than that from grain-fed cows.

TEXT-DEPENDENT QUESTIONS

1. What do all dairy foods have in common?
2. Name at least three dairy foods besides cow's milk.
3. Explain some of the differences between small and large animal farms.
4. What does it mean to process milk?
5. Why can milk be shipped over such long distances?

This is called ripening. Next, rennet is stirred into the mixture. Rennet is a substance that causes the milk to separate into curds and whey. The whey is liquid, and the curd becomes the cheese. The curds are separated from the whey, salted, and pressed into shapes.

After the cheese, yogurt, or ice cream is made, it has to be packaged. So does regular milk. Factories pour milk into cartons or jugs, wrap cheese, and package other dairy foods so they're ready to move on to stores.

FOR SALE

Dairy foods have to be shipped from factories to grocery stores. Trucks, trains, boats, or planes get the dairy foods to stores around the world. Because transportation is refrigerated, milk and dairy products can travel really long distances without spoiling.

Once they arrive at their grocery store destinations, store workers unpack them and put the products onto shelves. Most dairy products have pretty short **shelf lives** compared to some other foods. Milk will only stay good for a couple weeks, especially by the time it arrives at the store. Other dairy products, like cheese, will last longer.

Some dairy products aren't sold at grocery stores. You can sometimes buy them right from the farm that produces the milk. Some farms sell their milk, cheese, yogurt, and more at farmers' markets. Customers at farmers' markets can buy their food directly from farmers and those who make foods like dairy products.

But no matter where your dairy foods come from, you need to be sure to eat them every day!

WORDS TO UNDERSTAND

digestive system: The parts of your body that work together to break down food and take nutrients from it.

ligaments: The tough fibers that connect your bones together.

intolerant: Unable to digest something normally.

tendons: Tough bands that connect your muscles to your bones.

descent: Having to do with who your ancestors were.

Chapter

2

Why Do I Need to Eat Dairy Every Day?

People need to eat food for a couple reasons. One is energy. Without food, we wouldn't have any energy. And without energy, our bodies can't do anything. All foods, including dairy foods, provide energy.

Food also gives us nutrients. Nutrients keep the body healthy and working right. Without nutrients, we wouldn't be alive.

NUTRIENTS

Nutrients are tiny—so small that you can't see them when you look at food. But even though they're small, they're a very important part of food.

Some nutrients are macronutrients. People need to eat large amounts of macronutrients

MAKE CONNECTIONS

Vitamins and minerals are both types of nutrients necessary for health. They come from different sources, though. Vitamins are named A through K and are made by plants. People need to eat those plants (or the animals that eat them) to get those nutrients, since our bodies can't make them. Minerals are similar, but they aren't made by plants. They come from the ground. Plants suck minerals up from the soil, and when we eat those plants, we get those minerals. Vitamins and minerals are all part of a big food chain.

to stay healthy. The three kinds of macronutrients are fats, carbohydrates, and protein. Each of these macronutrients does specific things for the body. Fats protect organs and store energy for the long term. Carbohydrates provide most of our energy and keep the *digestive system* moving. Protein builds muscles and helps wounds and injuries heal.

Other nutrients are called micronutrients. People need to eat smaller amounts of micronutrients. Vitamins and minerals are micronutrients. Vitamins range from vitamin A through vitamin K. Each vitamin helps the body in a different way. For example, vitamin A is good for eye health and vision.

Minerals work the same way. Different minerals keep different parts of the body working right. Iron helps blood cells carry oxygen throughout the body. Magnesium helps protect bones. There are many kinds of minerals, and all are important!

THE NUTRIENTS IN DAIRY FOODS

Dairy foods are healthy, because they are high in many important nutrients. You may already be familiar with one—calcium. Other foods have calcium, but dairy foods have the most.

Calcium works to keep bones and teeth strong. Calcium is especially important for young people. During the early years of life, people's bodies build up bone mass. That's why kids are encouraged to drink so much milk.

Calcium makes bones thicker and stronger. Without enough calcium, bones become weak and brittle and break much more easily. Calcium also helps protect against a bone disease caused osteoporosis.

Dairy foods are high in plenty of other great nutrients, too. Protein is one. Protein makes muscles strong and repairs injured body tissues (like *tendons* and *ligaments*).

Dairy foods also have a mineral called potassium. Scientists think potassium keeps blood pressure healthy. High blood pressure can lead to health problems, like heart attacks, so having low blood pressure keeps you healthy in the future.

Milk and other dairy foods also have a lot of fat in them naturally. While fat is part of a healthy diet, too much fat may cause health problems. Healthier fats are called unsaturated

MAKE CONNECTIONS

You have a few choices when you buy milk, from whole to skim. These choices refer to how much fat is in the milk. Whole milk doesn't actually have 100 percent fat. It's made up of about 3 percent fat. The other 97 percent is water, milk sugar, and small amounts of other nutrients. Two percent milk is 2 percent fat, while 1 percent milk has 1 percent fat. Skim milk has no fat.

fats. They are found mostly in foods that come from plants. Saturated fats are less healthy and are found in foods that come from animals.

Dairy foods come from animals, and they can be high in saturated fats. Some nutritionists recommend people drink and eat dairy foods that are low fat or fat-free.

In general, if you eat a lot of foods with saturated fats in them—like meat, fried foods, and baked goods—you may want to think about drinking and eating dairy foods with lower amounts of fat in them. Instead of whole milk, try 2 percent, 1 percent, or skim. Skim milk has no fat in it at all.

Finally, milk is a good source of vitamin D. Like most foods, milk doesn't naturally have vitamin D in it. But factories add vitamin D, so people who drink milk can get this important nutrient. Vitamin D helps the body use calcium and keeps bones strong. Because it works with calcium, it makes sense that it's added to milk!

DAIRY ALTERNATIVES

Many people in the world can't digest milk. Their bodies don't digest milk sugar, called lactose. They are lactose *intolerant*. Their stomachs get upset if they drink milk or eat too many dairy foods.

There is nothing wrong with being lactose intolerant. In fact, up to 60 percent of everyone in the entire world is lactose intolerant!

For most of human history, people weren't able to digest lactose as adults. Babies could, of course, since they drank their mother's milk. But as babies grew up, they all lost the ability to digest the lactose as they switched to solid food.

However, a long time ago, some people started to be able to digest lactose. Their bodies were just accidentally different. Over time, those people had children and passed on the ability to digest lactose. Thousands of years later, many people now digest lactose as adults and drink milk regularly.

But not everyone. People of European descent are most likely to be able to drink milk and eat dairy foods. People of African, Asian, Latin American, and Native American *descent* are more likely to be lactose intolerant.

RESEARCH PROJECT

Dairy foods are important sources of calcium, but they are not the only sources. Do some research online to find out what other foods contain calcium. You may also want to look at food labels in your kitchen or where your family buys food. Write down the foods you're researching and how much calcium is found in each one, which you will most likely find in percentage form. Rank the foods you've researched. Which nondairy foods contain the most calcium? Which contain the least? As an extra step, do some research into how much calcium is in dairy foods. How does that compare to the calcium amounts you found in non-dairy foods?

Luckily for people who are lactose intolerant, there are lots of products made without lactose. You can even buy milk that has had the lactose removed!

TEXT-DEPENDENT QUESTIONS

1. What are the two main categories of nutrients? What is the difference between them?
2. How does calcium help your body stay healthy?
3. Name three nutrients besides calcium that are found in dairy foods.
4. Which kind of fat do scientists think is healthier? From where does it come?
5. According to the second side bar, what percentage of fat does whole milk contain? What about skim milk?

If you're lactose intolerant, you might still be able to eat some dairy foods. Cheese, yogurt, and butter have less lactose than milk. But some people who are lactose intolerant can't have any dairy products. They have to substitute other foods for dairy, because they aren't getting the calcium and other important nutrients found in dairy.

Lactose intolerant people can drink lactose-free milk. Or they can choose foods like spinach, fish, soymilk, and beans, which have calcium in them.

WORDS TO UNDERSTAND

routine: Something you do over and over the same way.

Chapter

3

So Why Can't I Just Eat Dairy Every Day?

Even though dairy foods are healthy, you can't just eat all dairy every day. You'd be missing out on many other important nutrients you can't get with dairy. Eating a wide variety of foods is key to being healthy.

MISSING NUTRIENTS

Dairy has calcium, some protein, fat, and some vitamin D. But what about all the other nutrients you need?

Dairy foods are missing key macronutrients like fiber. Fiber is a type of carbohydrate found in grains, vegetables, and fruits. The body doesn't actually digest fiber. But your body does need it to move food through your digestive system.

Important vitamins are also missing from dairy foods. Dairy doesn't have much of vitamins A, B, C, E, or K. Each of those vitamins is important for health. Without vitamin

Dairy foods are high in certain nutrients, but to get everything your body needs, you also need fruits, vegetables, proteins, and grains. It's best to eat lots of different kinds of food!

MAKE CONNECTIONS

You need so many nutrients, it's hard to keep track of them all! Here are a few of the big ones not found in high amounts in dairy:

- Vitamin A: Promotes vision and eye health.
- Vitamin B: Helps the body use energy.
- Vitamin C: Protects cells, helps wounds heal, and strengthens the immune system.
- Vitamin E: Protects cells and strengthens the immune system.
- Vitamin K: Helps blood clot to prevent bleeding.
- Magnesium: Makes up bones and teeth, keeps organs working right, helps produce energy.
- Iron: Allows red blood cells to carry oxygen to the rest of the body.
- Sodium: Keeps water levels in cells balanced.
- Zinc: Helps make new cells and aids in healing of wounds.

E, for example, your cells lack some protection from things like pollution and rays from the sun.

As far as minerals go, dairy foods lack iron, zinc, magnesium, and more. Without those minerals, your body will suffer, and you could get sick.

A BALANCED DIET

Luckily, there are plenty of available foods that aren't dairy! Dairy should definitely be part of your daily eating *routine*, but so should other healthy foods.

When you eat a wide variety of foods, you have a balanced diet. In this case, diet means the types and amounts of food you eat. It doesn't mean watching what you eat to lose weight.

One way to think about a balanced diet is to consider the five food groups. Food is grouped into five categories. Each of the foods in one category has similar nutrition to others in that group. Dairy foods are one food group. Dairy foods all come from animal milk and contain similar nutrients, like calcium.

The other food groups include fruit, vegetables, grains, and protein. Fruits and vegetables are plants that grow in the ground. They each have lots of vitamins and minerals. Many fruits, for instance, are high in vitamin C. Vegetables like spinach and kale have a lot of iron.

Grains are the seeds of certain grass plants. Rice, barley, wheat, and corn are all grains. They have a lot of carbohydrates, some protein, vitamin B, and many more vitamins and minerals.

RESEARCH PROJECT

Pick a nutrient listed in this chapter. It can be a nutrient found in dairy foods or in another food group. Become an expert on that nutrient. Research it online to find out where it comes from, how the body uses it, and what happens when people do not get enough of it. Write a short report about what you've learned.

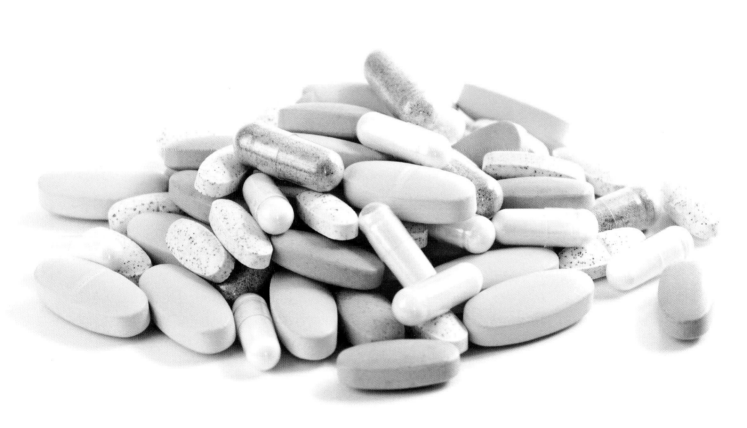

Sometimes, people have a hard time getting all the nutrients they need from food. When this happens, they can take special pills called vitamins or supplements, which provide some of what they're missing.

TEXT-DEPENDENT QUESTIONS

1. What are three nutrients dairy is missing?
2. According to the sidebar, what are 2 nutrients that strengthen the immune system?
3. Describe what a balanced diet is.
4. How many food groups are there? What are they?
5. How can you make sure you eat a balanced diet?

Protein foods are named for their main nutrient–protein. Meat, fish, eggs, beans, nuts, and seeds are all protein foods. Besides protein, these foods have iron, fat, and more.

When you regularly eat food from all five food groups, you have a balanced diet. If you only ate dairy every day, you'd be getting a lot of certain nutrients and almost none of others. A balanced diet means eating different kinds of foods to make sure your body gets the different nutrients it needs.

WORDS TO UNDERSTAND

equivalent: Something that works out to be about the same as something else.

quesadilla: A meal popular in Mexican food, made of a tortilla folded with melted cheese and other ingredients inside it.

Chapter

4

Putting Dairy on My Plate Every Day

Now it's time to turn ideas into action! Sure, it's important to eat dairy foods every day, but how do you actually go about doing that?

MYPLATE

An online tool called MyPlate can help you figure out how much dairy you need to eat or drink every day, and how to add it to your diet.

MyPlate was created by the U.S. Department of Agriculture (USDA). It is an image shaped like a plate divided into the five food groups. A website that goes along with My-Plate helps you figure out how to use the image in your everyday life.

Nutrition Facts

Serving Size 1 cup (228g)
Servings Per Container 2

Amount Per Serving

Calories 260 Calories from Fat 12

% Daily Valu

Total Fat 13g	20
Saturated Fat 5g	25
Cholesterol 30mg	10
Sodium 660mg	2
Total Carbohydrate 31g	1
Dietary Fiber 0g	

Nutrition facts labels are there to help you make better choices about the food you eat. It's easy to tell which foods have a lot of the things you want, like vitamins, minerals, and fiber—but you can also see which foods are high in fat or sodium, so you can avoid eating them too often.

MAKE CONNECTIONS

Yes, ice cream is a dairy food. It's made out of milk and does have some calcium and other good nutrients. It also has a lot of sugar, which makes it one of the least healthy dairy choices. An ice cream treat once in a while is OK, but don't count on ice cream to be your daily dairy food!

The MyPlate image is divided into four sections. On the right-hand side, it is divided in half for protein foods and grains. The left-hand side is divided into the bigger vegetable section and the smaller fruit section. In the upper-right corner is a glass, representing dairy.

The sections show you how much of each food group you should eat every day, compared with the other food groups. You should eat about the same amounts of protein, grains, fruits, and vegetables, but a little bit more vegetables and little less fruit. You should also drink a glass of milk or eat the *equivalent* amount of another dairy food, like cheese or yogurt.

You can use MyPlate to think about a single meal. For breakfast, you might have an omelet with peppers, tomatoes, and onions. You could also have some toast, a sliced apple, and a glass of milk. If you divided your breakfast into each food group, your plate would look a lot like MyPlate. The peppers, tomatoes, and onions would be in the vegetable section. The egg in your omelet would be in the protein section. The apple would be in the fruit section. The toast would be in the grain section. And the milk would be in the dairy section.

Since not all your meals always have all five food groups, imagine MyPlate holding the food you eat in a day. Over the three meals and any snacks you eat in a day, you should have a balance between all the food groups.

USING MYPLATE

MyPlate is even more useful if you understand how much of each food group you need to eat. The picture of the plate tells you how much of each you should eat in comparison with the other food groups. It doesn't tell you how much food you need to eat overall. If you ate a ton of food every day and it was all balanced like MyPlate shows, you might still not have a very healthy diet. You'd probably be eating way too much overall.

Luckily, the MyPlate website gives you all the information you need to eat healthfully. One of the things it tells you is how much dairy you should eat every day. The amount of dairy you eat depends on your age. Very young children ages two to three should get 2 cups of dairy a day. Children ages four to eight should eat 2½ cups of dairy a day. And everyone age nine or older should get 3 cups a day.

RESEARCH PROJECT

Use MyPlate to research another food group. You may choose fruit, vegetables, grains, or protein. Write a paragraph about what foods belong to your chosen food group. Next, write a paragraph about the nutrients found in that food group. Finally, research the amounts people should eat of that food group every day, and write a paragraph describing how much you should be eating based on your age and whether you're a girl or a boy.

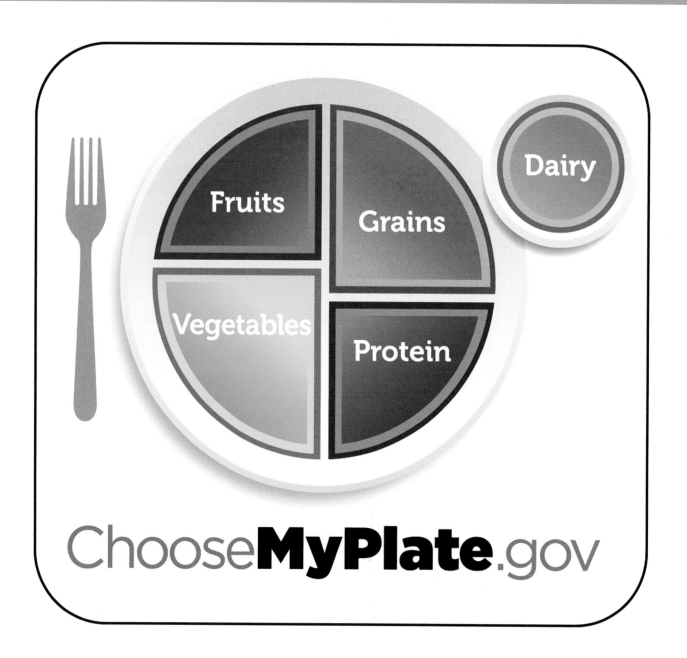

The USDA's MyPlate is designed to show how much of the food you eat should be from each food group. Whether you eat a lot or a little, about half of what you eat should be fruits and vegetables.

TEXT-DEPENDENT QUESTIONS

1. How many sections does MyPlate have? Why does it have that many?
2. Where is the dairy section found on MyPlate?
3. How many cups of dairy should a 5-year-old have? What about a 13-year-old?
4. How much shredded cheese equals 1 cup of dairy?
5. According to the sidebar, why shouldn't someone eat ice cream every day to get enough dairy?

One cup of dairy can mean several things. It could simply mean one cup (8 ounces) of milk. It also means one medium-sized cup of yogurt that contains 8 ounces. A third of a cup of shredded cheese counts at one cup of dairy; so does 1½ ounces of sliced cheese (2 to 3 slices). One cup of dairy equals 2 cups of cottage cheese. As for desserts, 1 cup of pudding, and 1½ cups of ice cream can be considered 1 cup of dairy.

So to get 3 cups of dairy in a day, you have many choices. You could have a glass of milk for breakfast, a yogurt for lunch, and some cheese and crackers for a snack. Or you could have yogurt and fruit with granola for breakfast, a glass of milk with lunch, and a cheese **quesadilla** for dinner (with some veggies and protein). It's up to you.

Chapter

5

Fast Foods, Snacks, and Dairy

Dairy isn't only something you eat for breakfast, lunch, and dinner at home. You can choose to eat and drink dairy at restaurants and between meals, too. Those are great ways to get more dairy foods into your diet every day.

EATING OUT

You probably won't find it too difficult to find dairy at most restaurants, but it can be a little tougher in fast-food restaurants. Many people stop by fast-food places for a quick, cheap, and tasty meal or snack. Unfortunately, most of the food in these restaurants is pretty unhealthy. But with a little searching, you'll be able to find some healthier options. Dairy is a good place to start.

Some fast-food restaurants offer milk as part of their kid's meals. Milk is a much healthier

Certain snacks, like chips, cheese puffs, or other munchies, have a lot of calories but no vitamins or minerals. Nutritionists call these "empty calories." They recommend that your snacks should be fruits, vegetables, or other nutrient-rich foods.

choice than soda. Soda has a lot of sugar in it, without any other nutrients. Milk has all the important dairy nutrients.

You'll probably be able to find some cheeses in fast-food restaurants, but make sure you're not going overboard. Too much cheese on a burger, pizza, or quesadilla adds too much fat and salt to your food. But a little bit can be good.

Order a yogurt parfait for a dairy boost. The best parfaits use fresh fruit, not fruit drenched in sugary syrup. You want to choose dairy options that won't sneak in a lot of sugar.

Other options you might find include bagels and cream cheese (be sure to get whole-wheat or whole-grain bagels) and smoothies made with milk or yogurt.

SNACKS

Dairy can also be part of healthy snacks. In general, snacks are great additions to a healthy diet. It all depends on the snacks you choose, though.

Unhealthy junk food snacks definitely aren't part of a healthy, balanced diet. It's all right to have chips, ice cream, and baked goods once in a while. But they aren't good choices for snacks every day.

The point of a snack is to give you enough energy between meals to keep yourself going. If you have hours and hours between lunch and dinner and need an energy boost, eat a snack! Snacks are smaller than main meals. They give you a boost of energy to get to the next meal. They don't replace a meal itself.

Snacks are also good ways to add in some extra nutrition to your diet. They can help you keep your diet balanced. If you've already eaten two meals in a day and haven't eaten any vegetables, eat a veggie snack, like celery and peanut butter. You'll be adding in the nutrients you need from vegetables.

You can do the same thing with dairy. If you haven't eaten enough dairy in a day, have a dairy snack! There are lots of possibilities, including:

* A smoothie made with fresh or frozen fruit and milk or yogurt
* Cheese and whole-wheat crackers

RESEARCH PROJECT

Do some research into your favorite fast-food restaurant's meals. Pick a restaurant and a meal from there that you've eaten before. Check online for nutrition information for each of the foods in that meal. You can also check to see if the restaurant has a brochure listing the nutrition information for the food it serves. You might find information on a kid's meal with a cheeseburger, french fries, and milk. Write down the nutrition information for the meal, including the amounts of sugar, salt (sodium), fat, protein, vitamins, and minerals. Do you think the meal you chose is healthy? Think of ways the restaurant could make it healthier.

Smoothies made with fresh berries are a great way to get a couple servings of fruit, all in one refreshing drink!

- Celery with cream cheese spread in the groove
- Freeze yogurt cups with popsicle sticks stuck in them to make frozen yogurt pops
- Shredded cheese (and vegetables) added to a tortilla, folded in half, and melted on the stovetop or in the microwave
- A yogurt dip with spices and herbs for vegetables or crackers, or a sweet version with honey to use for fruit
- Mozzarella balls and cherry tomatoes on toothpicks
- A glass of milk
- Mini pizzas made with whole-wheat English muffins, tomato sauce, and shredded cheese
- Mini whole-wheat bagels with cream cheese

You can see many of these snacks have more than just dairy in them. The best healthy snacks are made of more than one food group. Just make sure your snacks are low in sugar, salt, and unhealthy fat. Healthy snacks can be part of an overall healthy diet and a healthy life!

WORDS TO UNDERSTAND

circulatory system: Your heart and blood vessels, which work together to carry oxygen and nutrients all over your body.

developed countries: Countries with a strong economy. Developed countries usually have medical treatment, transportation, and jobs for almost all of their citizens.

side effects: Something else that happens after you take a drug or eat a food, besides the thing you wanted to happen.

nutritionists: People who are experts on healthy eating.

stroke: When a blood vessel in the brain bursts or is blocked, damaging the brain's ability to send and receive messages from the rest of the body.

Chapter
6

The Big Picture

Healthy eating is more than just following the instructions of adults who nag you to make better choices. Healthy eating is about taking care of yourself and making sure you stay well now and in the future. Healthy eating is an important part of the equation for good living.

Dairy has so many good nutrients that it's great for health in many ways. Your bones will be stronger because of the calcium and vitamin D in dairy. Your muscles will work right from the protein. Your blood pressure will stay low because of the potassium. All together, the nutrients in dairy keep your body working the way it should and keep you living your life the best way possible.

Other healthy foods do similar things. Dairy foods are just one part of overall healthy eating. Healthy eating has a lot of benefits, both now and for your future.

HEALTHY ENERGY AND WEIGHT

Of course, dairy isn't the only good food out there. Eating all the other food groups leads to health both today and tomorrow.

Eating a balanced diet is only one part of staying healthy. It's also important to be active. Exercise helps you burn off any extra calories, improves circulation, and strengthens your immune system!

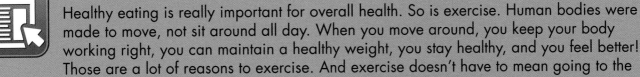

MAKE CONNECTIONS

Healthy eating is really important for overall health. So is exercise. Human bodies were made to move, not sit around all day. When you move around, you keep your body working right, you can maintain a healthy weight, you stay healthy, and you feel better! Those are a lot of reasons to exercise. And exercise doesn't have to mean going to the gym or running. Find an activity you like to do that gets you moving. You could join a sports team or take sports lessons. You could go for a walk or hike. You could play a game of basketball or soccer with friends. Try yoga, swimming, or dancing. The choices are endless! Whatever you choose, try to get at least an hour of exercise a day.

When you start practicing healthy eating habits, you notice the difference right away. For example, healthy food gives you lots of energy, which will keep you going the whole day.

If you eat too many unhealthy foods, you might not feel very well or very energetic. After eating a big, greasy meal, you might feel sluggish and tired. You don't really want to do anything but lie around. Maybe you have a stomachache. Or after eating a lot of sugar, you get a rush of sudden energy, but then crash a little while later and maybe get a headache.

Healthy foods give you energy that lasts longer and doesn't cause unpleasant **side effects**. After you eat a healthy-sized meal with lots of food groups and nutrients in it, you feel ready to take on the rest of the day. You won't feel bloated, tired, or achy. You'll just feel ready to go!

Healthy foods also help you have a healthy weight. Everyone has a different healthy weight. A healthy weight means your body is working right. It doesn't mean you look a certain way.

Several things go into having a healthy weight. First is eating the right amount of food. Someone with a healthy diet doesn't eat too much—or too little. She doesn't eat huge meals that make her stuffed three times a day. She also doesn't skip meals when she's hungry.

Eating the right kinds of foods is also necessary to a healthy weight. Eating junk food all the time makes many people gain weight. By choosing to eat healthy foods, you'll be making the choice to have a healthy weight.

AVOIDING ILLNESS

The list of good things that come from healthy eating is even longer. You'll also avoid many health problems and sicknesses by choosing to eat healthy amounts of healthy foods.

A lot of **nutritionists** talk about how healthy eating helps people keep from getting a serious illness in the future. But having a good diet also keeps you healthy right now. Many healthy foods strengthen the immune system, the body system that fights the germs that

People with diabetes often need to test their blood regularly to make sure their blood sugar levels are healthy. They might need to prick themselves like this every day—or more often.

RESEARCH PROJECT

Do some further research into osteoporosis, the bone disease partly caused by not getting enough dairy in your diet. Write a short report that answers the following questions: What is osteoporosis, and what are its symptoms? Who suffers most from this disease? How is it treated? Is osteoporosis preventable, and if so, how can it be avoided?

cause illnesses. Lots of nutrients, like vitamins C and E, make the immune system stronger. A stronger immune system means your body is better able to fight off bacteria and viruses that may make you sick.

As for the future, choosing to eat healthy foods now is one of the best things you can do to avoid serious illness and other health problems.

Dairy, in particular, helps prevent the bone disease osteoporosis. People with osteoporosis have weak bones that break easily. They suffer especially from broken hips, the spine, and the wrists. Luckily, a diet with a lot of calcium and having enough vitamin D in the body can reduce the risk of osteoporosis.

Healthy eating in general also prevents a wide range of health problems. Heart disease is a leading cause of death in the United States and other **developed countries**. Heart disease isn't always linked to diet, but it often is. Unhealthy diets full of fat and junk foods cause all sorts of problems with the **circulatory system**, including heart attacks and hardened arteries. Scientists think that avoiding unhealthy foods and eating healthy ones cuts the risk of heart disease by a whole lot.

Diabetes is another disease linked to unhealthy eating. Diabetes is a disease in which the body can't process sugar the way it should. A substance called insulin normally changes the sugar we eat into energy we can use. The body of someone with diabetes can't use insulin well.

People with type 1 diabetes don't produce insulin at all. They have to give themselves shots of insulin. Type 1 diabetes doesn't have anything to do with diet.

Diet can play a major role in type 2 diabetes, though. People with type 2 diabetes don't produce enough insulin and can't use the insulin properly. People who are overweight and eat unhealthy foods are at higher risk for diabetes than others.

Many, many people have diabetes. According to the American Diabetes Association (ADA), almost 26 million people in the United States have diabetes. Even young people have diabetes. The ADA estimates 215,000 people under the age of twenty have it. Not all of these people have type 2 diabetes, but the World Health Organization estimates that 90 percent of people with diabetes have type 2.

Diabetes is a dangerous disease. It can often be managed with a healthy diet and exercise.

Sometimes medication is necessary. Complications from diabetes aren't anything to laugh at. People with diabetes suffer from foot problems, eye problems, kidney disease, and hearing problems, among other things. Diabetes also leads to heart disease and **stroke**, which can cause death.

Fortunately, eating well can help prevent diabetes and many other diseases. Healthy eating and exercise reduces the risk of serious diseases and can keep you living a great life for a long time.

TAKING CONTROL

As a young person, it's up to you to make healthy choices. You may not always have the freedom to pick exactly the kinds of healthy foods you want to eat, but you do have some control. Your family and your school may put limits on the choices you have, but if you decide to eat healthier, you can make it happen.

If you get breakfast or lunch at school, make healthy choices. Choose a variety of food groups. Stay away from junk food. Don't just eat french fries or chips and soda for lunch. Make sure you choose fruits, vegetables, dairy, and the rest of the food groups.

At home, don't refuse to eat the healthier foods your family tries to put on your plate. Instead of turning up your nose at corn, try it! If you've never tried a healthy food, at least take a taste. You might like it. Even if you don't, keep trying. People sometimes need to try a new food a few times before they learn to like it.

Maybe your family doesn't serve very healthy food. Maybe your parents come home with fast-food takeout or serve TV dinners. Talk to your family members about picking healthier food. Even if your dad has to pick up takeout, you can figure out what the healthier options are.

By taking control of your eating habits now, you'll be doing yourself (and your family) a huge favor. You'll feel better, and you'll keep yourself healthy for the future.

Dairy is part of a healthy diet. Drinking milk or eating yogurt or cheese adds important nutrients, like calcium, to your life. From the farm to your table, dairy's journey to your stomach is a great way to start eating healthfully today!

Find Out More

ONLINE

Calcium
kidshealth.org/teen/food_fitness/nutrition/calcium.html

Dairy
www.choosemyplate.gov/food-groups/dairy.html

MyPlate Kids' Place
www.choosemyplate.gov/kids/index.html

Nourish Interactive
www.nourishinteractive.com

Where Is My Milk From?
www.whereismymilkfrom.com/#howitworks

IN BOOKS

Bingham, Jane. *Producing Dairy and Eggs*. North Mankato, Minn.: Heinemann-Raintree, 2012.

Graimes, Nicola. *Kids' Fun and Health Cookbook*. New York: DK Publishing, 2007.

Malam, John. *Journey of a Glass of Milk*. North Mankato, Minn.: Heinemann-Raintree, 2012.

Sertori, Trisha. *Dairy Foods (Body Fuel for Healthy Bodies)*. Pelham, N.Y.: Benchmark Books, 2008.

Spilsbury, Louise. *Milk and Dairy (Eat Smart)*. Portsmouth, N.H.: Heinemann, 2009.

Series Glossary of Key Terms

Carbohydrates: The types of molecules in food that we get most of our energy from. Foods like sugars and grains are especially high in carbohydrates.

Dairy: Milk or foods that are made from milk.

Diabetes: A disease where the body can't use sugar to produce energy correctly.

Diet: All the foods and nutrients that you normally eat.

Energy: The power stored in food that lets your body move around and carry out other body functions.

Farm: A place where plants and animals are grown and raised to produce food.

Fast food: Food designed to be ready for the customer as fast as possible. Usually it's more expensive and less healthy than fresh food, but it is very convenient.

Fiber: Tough parts of plant foods that your body can't digest. Fiber helps your digestive system function normally.

Fruits: A food group that includes the edible parts of plants that contain the seeds. They are often colorful and have a sweet flavor.

Grains: The seeds of various kinds of grass plants. Grains include rice, wheat, corn, and many others. They are high in carbohydrates and fiber, and can be stored for a long time.

Harvest: The process of gathering crops or the time when crops are gathered.

Local foods: Foods that are grown close to where they are eaten, so they don't have to be transported very far.

Minerals: Materials found naturally in metals or rocks. Our bodies need certain minerals in very small quantities.

Nutrients: Any part of food that our body uses in some way to survive and stay healthy.

Obesity: A state of being so overweight that it's bad for your health.

Organic: A way of producing food in which no genetic modifications, harmful pesticides, or hormones can be used.

Protein: The chemical parts of food that your body uses to build muscles and perform certain body processes. If your body runs out of carbohydrates and fat, it will start using protein for energy.

Vegetables: Plant foods that are usually made of the flower, stem, leaf, or root of a plant. They are usually high in fiber and certain nutrients.

Vitamins: Certain kinds of molecules that your body cannot produce. Instead, you need to get them in your diet to stay healthy.

Index

About the Author & Consultant

Rosa Waters lives in New York State. She has worked as a writer for several years, producing works on health, history, and other topics.

Dr. Lisa Prock is a developmental behavioral pediatrician at Children's Hospital (Boston) and Harvard Medical School. She attended college at the University of Chicago, medical school at Columbia University, and received a master's degree in public health from the Harvard School of Public Health. Board-certified in general pediatrics and developmental behavioral pediatrics, she currently is Clinical Director of Developmental and Behavioral Pediatrics and Consultant to the Walker School, a residential school serving children in foster care. Dr. Prock has combined her clinical interests in child development and international health with advocacy for children in medical, residential, and educational settings since 1991. She has worked in Cambodia teaching pediatrics and studying tuberculosis epidemiology; and in Eastern Europe visiting children with severe neurodevelopmental challenges in orphanages. She has co-authored numerous original publications and articles for families. She is a also nonprofit board member for organizations and has received numerous local and national awards for her work with children and families.

Picture Credits